Simplicity
Journal

BARBOUR
PUBLISHING

Compiled by Kathy Shutt.

ISBN 978-1-60260-850-4

Quotes beginning with the words "Simple pleasures like. . ." or "A simple pleasure like. . ." are written by Joanie Garborg.

Scripture quotations marked NLT are taken from the *Holy Bible*, New Living Translation, copyright © 1996, 2004. Used by permission of Tyndale House Publishers, Inc. Wheaton, Illinois 60189, U.S.A. All rights reserved.

Scripture quotations marked MSG are from *THE MESSAGE*. Copyright © by Eugene H. Peterson 1993, 1994, 1995, 1996, 2000, 2001, 2002. Used by permission of NavPress Publishing Group.

Scripture quotations marked NIV are taken from the HOLY BIBLE, NEW INTERNATIONAL VERSION®. NIV®. Copyright © 1973, 1978, 1984 by International Bible Society. Used by permission of Zondervan. All rights reserved.

Scripture quotations marked KJV are taken from the King James Version of the Bible.

Published by Barbour Publishing, Inc., P.O. Box 719, Uhrichsville, Ohio 44683
www.barbourbooks.com

Our mission is to publish and distribute inspirational products offering exceptional value and biblical encouragement to the masses.

Member of the
Evangelical Christian
Publishers Association

Printed in China.

*N*othing is worth more than this day.
JOHANN WOLFGANG VON GOETHE

I would rather be able to appreciate things I cannot have than to have things I am not able to appreciate.

ELBERT HUBBARD

Date and Time:

Place:

Today, I found simple inspiration in:

Other inspiring thoughts: _____

_____

_____

_____

_____

_____

_____

_____

_____

_____

_____

_____

_____

_____

_____

_____

_____

_____

_____

*All the beautiful sentiments in the world
weigh less than a simple lovely action.*
JAMES RUSSELL LOWELL

*Simple pleasures like fluffy towels fresh from
the dryer caress us with fragrant, sumptuous warmth.*

Date and Time:

Place:

Today, I found simple inspiration in:

Other inspiring thoughts: _____

_____

_____

_____

_____

_____

_____

_____

_____

_____

_____

_____

_____

_____

_____

_____

_____

_____

_____

_____

_____

*Living the truth in your heart without
compromise brings kindness into the world.*
EIGHTEENTH CENTURY MONK

You're my place of quiet retreat;
I wait for your Word to renew me. . . .
Therefore I lovingly embrace everything you say.
PSALM 119:114, 119 MSG

Date and Time:

Place:

Today, I found simple inspiration in:

Other inspiring thoughts: _____

_____

_____

_____

_____

_____

_____

_____

_____

_____

_____

_____

_____

_____

_____

_____

_____

_____

_____

Jesus—
Light of the world.
Joy of our hearts.
UNKNOWN

Add to your joy by counting your blessings.

UNKNOWN

Date and Time:

Place:

Today, I found simple inspiration in:

Other inspiring thoughts: _____

_____

_____

_____

_____

_____

_____

_____

_____

_____

_____

_____

_____

_____

_____

_____

_____

_____

_____

_____

_____

*A simple pleasure like the laughter of children shimmers
with the infectious joy of hearts that truly believe.*

When things are complicated, I wish you simple beauty;
When things are chaotic, I wish you inner silence;
When things seem empty, I wish you hope and joy.

UNKNOWN

Date and Time:

Place:

Today, I found simple inspiration in:

Other inspiring thoughts: _____

_____

_____

_____

_____

_____

_____

_____

_____

_____

_____

_____

_____

_____

_____

_____

_____

_____

_____

_____

_____

Wishing you all the simple pleasures in life
and the time in which to enjoy them.
UNKNOWN

Act with God in the greatest simplicity. Speak to Him frankly and plainly. Implore His assistance in your affairs just as they are happening: He will never fail to grant it.

BROTHER LAWRENCE

Date and Time:

Place:

Today, I found simple inspiration in:

Other inspiring thoughts: _____

_____

_____

_____

_____

_____

_____

_____

_____

_____

_____

_____

_____

_____

_____

_____

_____

_____

_____

*Simple pleasures like Sunday morning hymns
raise our spirits in anthems of exultant praise.*

*Take your everyday, ordinary life—your sleeping,
eating, going-to-work, and walking-around life—
and place it before God as an offering. Embracing what
God does for you is the best thing you can do for him.*

ROMANS 12:1 MSG

Date and Time:

Place:

Today, I found simple inspiration in:

Other inspiring thoughts: _____

_____

_____

_____

_____

_____

_____

_____

_____

_____

_____

_____

_____

_____

_____

_____

_____

_____

_____

_____

*God loves us, and the will of love is always
blessing for its loved ones.*
HANNAH WHITALL SMITH

Do a deed of simple kindness;
Though its end you may not see,
It may reach, like a widening ripple,
Down a long eternity.

JOSEPH PARKER NORRIS

Date and Time:

Place:

Today, I found simple inspiration in:

Other inspiring thoughts: _____

_____

_____

_____

_____

_____

_____

_____

_____

_____

_____

_____

_____

_____

_____

_____

_____

_____

_____

_____

_____

The patterns of our days are always changing. . .
rearranging. . .and each design for living is unique. . .
graced with its own special beauty.
UNKNOWN

"I have loved you with an everlasting love;
I have drawn you with loving-kindness."

JEREMIAH 31:3 NIV

Date and Time:

Place:

Today, I found simple inspiration in:

Other inspiring thoughts: _____

_____

_____

_____

_____

_____

_____

_____

_____

_____

_____

_____

_____

_____

_____

_____

_____

_____

_____

_____

*A simple pleasure like a beautiful package
excites anticipation. . .but the most
precious gifts are wrapped in love.*

*A simple pleasure like a starry twilight evening
reminds us that the One who created
such beauty also fashioned us.*

Date and Time:

Place:

Today, I found simple inspiration in:

Other inspiring thoughts: _____

_____

_____

_____

_____

_____

_____

_____

_____

_____

_____

_____

_____

_____

_____

_____

_____

_____

_____

_____

We may. . .depend upon God's promises,
for. . .He will be as good as His word.
He is so kind that He cannot deceive us,
so true that He cannot break His promise.
MATTHEW HENRY

"Oh, that we might know the LORD!
Let us press on to know him. He will respond to us as surely
as the arrival of dawn or the coming of rains in early spring."
HOSEA 6:3 NLT

Date and Time:

Place:

Today, I found simple inspiration in:

Other inspiring thoughts: _____

_____

_____

_____

_____

_____

_____

_____

_____

_____

_____

_____

_____

_____

_____

_____

_____

_____

_____

_____

*The simplest and commonest truth seems new
and wonderful when we experience it
for the first time in our own life.*
MARIE VON EBNER-ESCHENBACH

A simple pleasure like a birthday card celebrates the gift of living exuberantly, blessed by God.

Date and Time:

Place:

Today, I found simple inspiration in:

Other inspiring thoughts: _____

_____
_____
_____
_____
_____
_____
_____
_____
_____
_____
_____
_____
_____
_____
_____
_____
_____
_____
_____
_____

Where others see but the dawn coming over the hill,
I see the soul of God shouting for joy.
WILLIAM BLAKE

*May the God of hope fill you with all joy
and peace as you trust in him, so that you may
overflow with hope by the power of the Holy Spirit.*
ROMANS 15:13 NIV

Date and Time:

Place:

Today, I found simple inspiration in:

Other inspiring thoughts: _____

_____

_____

_____

_____

_____

_____

_____

_____

_____

_____

_____

_____

_____

_____

_____

_____

_____

_____

_____

_____

*Simple pleasures like star constellations sparkle
in silent testimony to God's creative love.*

*There's surely something charming in seeing the smallest
thing done so thoroughly, as if to remind the careless
that whatever is worth doing is worth doing well.*

CHARLES DICKENS

Date and Time:

Place:

Today, I found simple inspiration in:

Other inspiring thoughts: _____

_____

_____

_____

_____

_____

_____

_____

_____

_____

_____

_____

_____

_____

_____

_____

_____

_____

_____

_____

_____

A simple pleasure like birds singing lifts a chorus of gratitude to the heavenly Father who cares for us all.

Your life is hid with Christ in God.

COLOSSIANS 3:3 KJV

Date and Time:

Place:

Today, I found simple inspiration in:

Other inspiring thoughts: _____

_____

_____

_____

_____

_____

_____

_____

_____

_____

_____

_____

_____

_____

_____

_____

_____

_____

_____

_____

_____

_____

God writes the gospel not in the Bible alone,
but on trees and flowers and clouds and stars.
MARTIN LUTHER

In all ranks of life the human heart yearns
for the beautiful; and the beautiful things
that God makes are His gift to all alike.
HARRIET BEECHER STOWE

Date and Time:

Place:

Today, I found simple inspiration in:

Other inspiring thoughts: _____

_____

_____

_____

_____

_____

_____

_____

_____

_____

_____

_____

_____

_____

_____

_____

_____

_____

_____

_____

All our actions take their hue from the complexion
of the heart, as landscapes their variety from light.
FRANCIS BACON

I'm asking God for one thing, only one thing:
to live with him in his house my whole life long.
I'll contemplate his beauty; I'll study at his feet.
That's the only quiet, secure place in a noisy world.

PSALM 27:4–5 MSG

Date and Time:

Place:

Today, I found simple inspiration in:

Other inspiring thoughts: _____

_____

_____

_____

_____

_____

_____

_____

_____

_____

_____

_____

_____

_____

_____

_____

_____

_____

_____

_____

_____

_____

Simple pleasures like old photos capture images to be cherished and tucked away in the albums of our memories.

There is a silence into which the world cannot intrude.
There is a sacred peace you carry
in your heart and cannot lose.

UNKNOWN

Date and Time:

Place:

Today, I found simple inspiration in:

Other inspiring thoughts: _____

_____

_____

_____

_____

_____

_____

_____

_____

_____

_____

_____

_____

_____

_____

_____

_____

_____

_____

_____

_____

Before me, even as behind, God is, and all is well.
JOHN GREENLEAF WHITTIER

*Search high and low, scan skies and land,
you'll find nothing and no one quite like GOD. . . .
He looms immense and august over everyone around him.*

PSALM 89:6–7 MSG

Date and Time:

Place:

Today, I found simple inspiration in:

Other inspiring thoughts: _____

_____

_____

_____

_____

_____

_____

_____

_____

_____

_____

_____

_____

_____

_____

_____

_____

_____

_____

_____

_____

This is my Father's world: He shines in all that's fair;
In the rustling grass I hear Him pass;
He speaks to me everywhere.
MALTBIE D. BABCOCK

Simple pleasures like fleecy white clouds delight us with ever-changing images floating across azure skies.

Date and Time:

Place:

Today, I found simple inspiration in:

Other inspiring thoughts: _____

_____

_____

_____

_____

_____

_____

_____

_____

_____

_____

_____

_____

_____

_____

_____

_____

_____

_____

_____

_____

_____

The more I study nature,
the more I am amazed at the Creator.
LOUIS PASTEUR

But what happens when we live God's way?
He brings gifts into our lives, much the same way
that fruit appears in an orchard—things like affection
for others, exuberance about life, serenity.

GALATIANS 5:22 MSG

Date and Time:

Place:

Today, I found simple inspiration in:

Other inspiring thoughts: _____

_____

_____

_____

_____

_____

_____

_____

_____

_____

_____

_____

_____

_____

_____

_____

_____

_____

_____

_____

*A simple pleasure like birds building a nest
gives us hope for our own fresh beginnings.*

Our Lord does not care so much for the importance of our works as for the love with which they are done.

TERESA OF AVILA

Date and Time:

Place:

Today, I found simple inspiration in:

Other inspiring thoughts: _____

_____

_____

_____

_____

_____

_____

_____

_____

_____

_____

_____

_____

_____

_____

_____

_____

_____

_____

Each little flower that opens, each little bird that sings,
God made their glowing colors, He made their tiny wings.
CECIL FRANCES ALEXANDER

Date and Time:

Place:

Today, I found simple inspiration in:

Other inspiring thoughts: _____

_____

_____

_____

_____

_____

_____

_____

_____

_____

_____

_____

_____

_____

_____

_____

_____

_____

_____

_____

_____

*To be glad of life, because it gives you the chance to love
and to work and to play and to look up at the stars; to be satisfied
with your possessions. . .to think seldom of your enemies, often of
your friends, and every day of Christ; and to spend as much time
as you can, with body and with spirit in God's out-of-doors—
these are little guideposts on the footpath to peace.*

HENRY VAN DYKE

Date and Time:

Place:

Today, I found simple inspiration in:

Other inspiring thoughts: _____

_____

_____

_____

_____

_____

_____

_____

_____

_____

_____

_____

_____

_____

_____

_____

_____

_____

_____

_____

_____

*As we grow in our capacities to discover the joys
that God has placed in our lives, life becomes a
glorious experience of discovering His endless wonders.*
UNKNOWN

"Be still, and know that I am God."
PSALM 46:10 NIV

Date and Time:

Place:

Today, I found simple inspiration in:

Other inspiring thoughts: _____

_____

_____

_____

_____

_____

_____

_____

_____

_____

_____

_____

_____

_____

_____

_____

_____

_____

_____

_____

_____

A simple pleasure like a bubble bath pampers us with sweet-scented foam and soothes us with luxuriant tranquility.

I have learned to live each day as it comes,
and not to borrow trouble by dreading tomorrow.

DOROTHY DIX

Date and Time:

Place:

Today, I found simple inspiration in:

Other inspiring thoughts: _____

_____

_____

_____

_____

_____

_____

_____

_____

_____

_____

_____

_____

_____

_____

_____

_____

_____

*Let me, if I may, be ever welcomed to my room in winter
by a glowing hearth, in summer by a vase of flowers; if I may not,
let me think how nice they would be, and bury myself in my work.
I do not think that the road to contentment lies in despising
what we have not got. Let us acknowledge all good,
all delight that the world holds, and be content.*
GEORGE MACDONALD

The best things are nearest: breath in your nostrils,
light in your eyes, flowers at your feet,
duties at your hand, the path of God just before you.

ROBERT LOUIS STEVENSON

Date and Time:

Place:

Today, I found simple inspiration in:

Other inspiring thoughts: _____

_____

_____

_____

_____

_____

_____

_____

_____

_____

_____

_____

_____

_____

_____

_____

_____

_____

_____

*I want you woven into a tapestry of love, in touch with
everything there is to know of God. Then you will have minds confident
and at rest, focused on Christ, God's great mystery.
All the richest treasures of wisdom and knowledge are
embedded in that mystery and nowhere else.*

COLOSSIANS 2:2–3 MSG

A simple pleasure like a steaming cup of tea infuses the moment with peace and allows us to savor our blessings.

Date and Time:

Place:

Today, I found simple inspiration in:

Other inspiring thoughts: _____

_____

_____

_____

_____

_____

_____

_____

_____

_____

_____

_____

_____

_____

_____

_____

_____

_____

_____

_____

True silence is the rest of the mind; it is to the spirit what
sleep is to the body—nourishment and refreshment.
WILLIAM PENN

> *"Let the beloved of the Lord rest secure in him,*
> *for he shields him all day long, and the one*
> *the Lord loves rests between his shoulders."*
> DEUTERONOMY 33:12 NIV

Date and Time: _____

Place: _____

Today, I found simple inspiration in: _____

Other inspiring thoughts: _____

_____

_____

_____

_____

_____

_____

_____

_____

_____

_____

_____

_____

_____

_____

_____

_____

_____

_____

To think of [God's] rest is to give rest to the soul.
BERNARD OF CLAIRVAUX

A simple pleasure like a cool ocean breeze
blowing across the vast expanse of waters reminds us
that even in God's immensity, He is mindful of us.

Date and Time:

Place:

Today, I found simple inspiration in:

Other inspiring thoughts: _____

_____

_____

_____

_____

_____

_____

_____

_____

_____

_____

_____

_____

_____

_____

_____

_____

_____

_____

If we learn how to give of ourselves, to forgive others,
and to live with thanksgiving, we need not seek happiness.
It will seek us.

UNKNOWN

> "*Peace I leave with you; my peace I give you.*
> *I do not give to you as the world gives.*
> *Do not let your hearts be troubled and do not be afraid.*"
>
> JOHN 14:27 NIV

Date and Time:

Place:

Today, I found simple inspiration in:

Other inspiring thoughts: _____

_____

_____

_____

_____

_____

_____

_____

_____

_____

_____

_____

_____

_____

_____

_____

_____

_____

_____

_____

_____

*Doing little things with a strong desire
to please God makes them really great.*
FRANCIS DE SALES

I'll tell you how the sun rose—
one ribbon at a time.
EMILY DICKINSON

Date and Time:

Place:

Today, I found simple inspiration in:

Other inspiring thoughts: _____

_____

_____

_____

_____

_____

_____

_____

_____

_____

_____

_____

_____

_____

_____

_____

_____

_____

_____

_____

*A simple pleasure like a butterfly on the wing
inspires our spirits to soar toward
the Creator of such intricate beauty.*

"My Presence will go with you,
and I will give you rest."
EXODUS 33:14 NIV

Date and Time:

Place:

Today, I found simple inspiration in:

Other inspiring thoughts: _____

_____

_____

_____

_____

_____

_____

_____

_____

_____

_____

_____

_____

_____

_____

_____

_____

_____

_____

_____

_____

*If the day and the night are such that you greet them
with joy, and life emits a fragrance like flowers
and sweet-scented herbs, is more elastic, more starry,
more immortal—that is your success.*

HENRY DAVID THOREAU

Teach me the art of creating islands of stillness,
in which I can absorb the beauty of everyday things:
clouds, trees, a snatch of music. . .
MARION STROUD

Date and Time:

Place:

Today, I found simple inspiration in:

Other inspiring thoughts: _____

_____

_____

_____

_____

_____

_____

_____

_____

_____

_____

_____

_____

_____

_____

_____

_____

_____

_____

_____

_____

I can see how it might be possible for a man to look down upon the earth and be an atheist, but I cannot conceive how he could look up into the heavens and say there is no God.

ABRAHAM LINCOLN

Let the heavens be glad, and the earth rejoice! . . .
Let the sea and everything in it shout his praise! . . .
Let the trees of the forest rustle with praise. . . . Give thanks
to the LORD, for he is good! His faithful love endures forever.

1 CHRONICLES 16:31–34 NLT

Date and Time:

Place:

Today, I found simple inspiration in:

Other inspiring thoughts: _____

_____

_____

_____

_____

_____

_____

_____

_____

_____

_____

_____

_____

_____

_____

_____

_____

_____

_____

_____

*The light of God's presence is seen plainest
when all around is dark.*
UNKNOWN

Simple pleasures like cardinals in winter
symbolize that though our sins are as scarlet,
Jesus can make us whiter than snow.

Date and Time:

Place:

Today, I found simple inspiration in:

Other inspiring thoughts: _____

_____

_____

_____

_____

_____

_____

_____

_____

_____

_____

_____

_____

_____

_____

_____

_____

_____

_____

_____

All that is good, all that is true, all that is beautiful,
all that is beneficent, be it great or small,
be it perfect or fragmentary, natural as well as supernatural,
moral as well as material, comes from God.
JOHN NEWMAN

He. . .crowns me with love and tender mercies.
He fills my life with good things.

PSALM 103:4–5 NLT

Date and Time:

Place:

Today, I found simple inspiration in:

Other inspiring thoughts: _____

_____

_____

_____

_____

_____

_____

_____

_____

_____

_____

_____

_____

_____

_____

_____

_____

_____

_____

_____

The best thing to give to your enemy is forgiveness; to an opponent, tolerance; to a friend, your heart; to your child, a good example. . .to yourself, respect; to all. . .charity.

LORD BALFOUR

*A simple pleasure like a purring cat
embraces us with deep contentment and recognition
of the treasure in the commonplace.*

Date and Time:

Place:

Today, I found simple inspiration in:

Other inspiring thoughts:

_Between the house and the store there are little pockets
of happiness. A bird, a garden, a friend's greeting,
a child's smile, a cat in the sunshine needing a stroke.
Recognize them or ignore them. It's always up to you._

PAM BROWN

The heavens proclaim the glory of God.
The skies display his craftsmanship.

PSALM 19:1 NLT

Date and Time:

Place:

Today, I found simple inspiration in:

Other inspiring thoughts: _____

_____

_____

_____

_____

_____

_____

_____

_____

_____

_____

_____

_____

_____

_____

_____

_____

_____

_____

_____

I believe that in each little thing created by God there is more than what is understood, even if it is a little ant.

TERESA OF AVILA

A simple pleasure like a pair of warm mittens spreads toasty comfort to our hearts as well as to our hands.

Date and Time:

Place:

Today, I found simple inspiration in:

Other inspiring thoughts:

For God is sheer beauty, all-generous in love,
loyal always and ever.
PSALM 100:5 MSG

Date and Time:

Place:

Today, I found simple inspiration in:

Other inspiring thoughts: _____

_____

_____

_____

_____

_____

_____

_____

_____

_____

_____

_____

_____

_____

_____

_____

_____

_____

_____

Some gifts are big, others are small.
Gifts from the heart are the best gifts of all.

UNKNOWN

*Yesterday is gone. Tomorrow has not yet come.
We have only today. Let us begin.*

MOTHER TERESA

Date and Time:

Place:

Today, I found simple inspiration in:

Other inspiring thoughts: _____

_____

_____

_____

_____

_____

_____

_____

_____

_____

_____

_____

_____

_____

_____

_____

_____

_____

_____

_____

_____

> *Do not let trifles disturb your tranquility of mind. . . .*
> *Life is too precious to be sacrificed for the nonessential*
> *and transient. . . . Ignore the inconsequential.*
>
> GRENVILLE KLEISER

God is good to one and all;
everything he does is suffused with grace.

PSALM 145:9 MSG

Date and Time:

Place:

Today, I found simple inspiration in:

Other inspiring thoughts: _____

_____

_____

_____

_____

_____

_____

_____

_____

_____

_____

_____

_____

_____

_____

_____

_____

_____

_____

_____

_____

_____

*Allow yourself some time for silence.
Simply being before God will regenerate your spirit.*
UNKNOWN

The Lord gives you the experience of enjoying His presence.
He touches you, and His touch is so delightful that,
more than ever, you are drawn inwardly to Him.

JEANNE GUYON

Date and Time:

Place:

Today, I found simple inspiration in:

Other inspiring thoughts: _____

_____

_____

_____

_____

_____

_____

_____

_____

_____

_____

_____

_____

_____

_____

_____

_____

_____

_____

_____

Simple pleasures like giant snowflakes remind us that we are unique in all of God's creations.

Love. . .puts up with anything, trusts God always,
always looks for the best, never looks back,
but keeps going to the end.
1 Corinthians 13:4, 7 msg

Date and Time:

Place:

Today, I found simple inspiration in:

Other inspiring thoughts: _____

_____

_____

_____

_____

_____

_____

_____

_____

_____

_____

_____

_____

_____

_____

_____

_____

_____

_____

_____

Cheerfulness brings sunshine to the soul and drives away the shadows of anxiety. To be cheerful under all circumstances is to radiate faith. It is an expression of hope and an attitude of joyful expectancy. . . . It is to know that God holds all things in His control and that He neither slumbers nor sleeps.

HANNAH WHITALL SMITH

*Every moment is full of wonder
and God is always present.*

UNKNOWN

Date and Time:

Place:

Today, I found simple inspiration in:

Other inspiring thoughts: _____

_____

_____

_____

_____

_____

_____

_____

_____

_____

_____

_____

_____

_____

_____

_____

_____

_____

_____

_____

_____

_____

Peace is the fairest form of happiness.
WILLIAM ELLERY CHANNING

*Anyone who wants to approach God
must believe both that he exists and that he cares
enough to respond to those who seek him.*

Date and Time:

Place:

Today, I found simple inspiration in:

Other inspiring thoughts: _____

_____

_____

_____

_____

_____

_____

_____

_____

_____

_____

_____

_____

_____

_____

_____

_____

_____

_____

_____

*Thanksgiving puts power in living, because it opens
the generators of the heart to respond gratefully,
to receive joyfully, and to react creatively.*

UNKNOWN

God, of Your goodness give me Yourself,
for You are enough for me.
And only in You do I have everything.

JULIAN OF NORWICH

Date and Time:

Place:

Today, I found simple inspiration in:

Other inspiring thoughts: _____

_____

_____

_____

_____

_____

_____

_____

_____

_____

_____

_____

_____

_____

_____

_____

_____

_____

_____

_____

_____

*For health and food, for love and friends, for everything
Thy goodness sends, Father in Heaven, we thank Thee.*

RALPH WALDO EMERSON

You have made known to me the paths of life;
you will fill me with joy in your presence.

ACTS 2:28 NIV

Date and Time:

Place:

Today, I found simple inspiration in:

Other inspiring thoughts:

_____

_____

_____

_____

_____

_____

_____

_____

_____

_____

_____

_____

_____

_____

_____

_____

_____

_____

_____

_____

_____

Calm me, O Lord, as you stilled the storm;
Still me, O Lord, keep me from harm.
Let all the tumult within me cease;
Enfold me, Lord, in your peace.
CELTIC TRADITIONAL

*A simple pleasure like a baby's innocence softens
our hearts and inspires childlike faith.*

Date and Time:

Place:

Today, I found simple inspiration in:

Other inspiring thoughts: _____

_____

_____

_____

_____

_____

_____

_____

_____

_____

_____

_____

_____

_____

_____

_____

_____

_____

_____

_____

*Seeing our Father in everything makes life
one long thanksgiving and gives a rest of heart.*
HANNAH WHITALL SMITH

"For in [Christ] we live and move and have our being."
ACTS 17:28 NIV

Date and Time:

Place:

Today, I found simple inspiration in:

Other inspiring thoughts: _____

_____

_____

_____

_____

_____

_____

_____

_____

_____

_____

_____

_____

_____

_____

_____

_____

_____

_____

_____

_____

There is no season such delight can bring,
As summer, autumn, winter, and the spring.
WILLIAM BROWNE

The key to happiness belongs to everyone on Earth
who recognizes simple things
as treasures of great worth.
UNKNOWN

Date and Time:

Place:

Today, I found simple inspiration in:

Other inspiring thoughts: _____

_____

_____

_____

_____

_____

_____

_____

_____

_____

_____

_____

_____

_____

_____

_____

_____

_____

_____

_____

Gratitude is the inward feeling of kindness received.
Thankfulness is the natural impulse to express that feeling.
Thanksgiving is the following of that impulse.
HENRY VAN DYKE

Date and Time:

Place:

Today, I found simple inspiration in:

Other inspiring thoughts: _____

_____

_____

_____

_____

_____

_____

_____

_____

_____

_____

_____

_____

_____

_____

_____

_____

_____

_____

_____

_____

Thou who hast given so much to me,
give one more thing—a grateful heart.

GEORGE HERBERT

*A simple pleasure like an evening on the front porch
opens our hearts to love our neighbor as ourselves.*

Date and Time:

Place:

Today, I found simple inspiration in:

Other inspiring thoughts: _____

_____

_____

_____

_____

_____

_____

_____

_____

_____

_____

_____

_____

_____

_____

_____

_____

_____

_____

*Gratitude consists in a watchful, minute attention to the
particulars of our state, and to the multitude of God's gifts,
taken one by one. It fills us with a consciousness
that God loves and cares for us,
even to the least event and smallest need of life.*
HENRY EDWARD MANNING

Real wisdom, God's wisdom, begins with a holy life
and is characterized by getting along with others.
It is gentle and reasonable, overflowing with mercy and blessings.

JAMES 3:17 MSG

Date and Time:

Place:

Today, I found simple inspiration in:

Other inspiring thoughts: _____

_____

_____

_____

_____

_____

_____

_____

_____

_____

_____

_____

_____

_____

_____

_____

_____

_____

_____

_____

_____

Nothing can separate you from His love, absolutely nothing. . . .
God is enough for time, and God is enough for eternity.
God is enough!
HANNAH WHITALL SMITH

The private and personal blessings we enjoy deserve the thanksgiving of a whole life.

JEREMY TAYLOR

Date and Time:

Place:

Today, I found simple inspiration in:

Other inspiring thoughts:

A simple pleasure like the smell of fresh-baked bread
can satisfy more than physical hunger.

> *"The LORD bless you and keep you; the LORD make his face shine upon you and be gracious to you; the LORD turn his face toward you and give you peace."*
>
> NUMBERS 6:24–26 NIV

Date and Time:

Place:

Today, I found simple inspiration in:

Other inspiring thoughts: _____

_____

_____

_____

_____

_____

_____

_____

_____

_____

_____

_____

_____

_____

_____

_____

_____

_____

_____

_____

_____

*Love brings a new richness to life,
a higher intensity, a deeper meaning.*

UNKNOWN

Gratitude is the homage of the heart,
rendered to God for His goodness.
NATHANIEL PARKER WILLIS

Date and Time:

Place:

Today, I found simple inspiration in:

Other inspiring thoughts: _____

_____

_____

_____

_____

_____

_____

_____

_____

_____

_____

_____

_____

_____

_____

_____

_____

_____

_____

_____

_____

Every single act of love bears the imprint of God.
UNKNOWN

Live a life worthy of the calling you have received.
Be completely humble and gentle; be patient,
bearing with one another in love.

EPHESIANS 4:1–2 NIV

Date and Time:

Place:

Today, I found simple inspiration in:

Other inspiring thoughts: _____

_____

_____

_____

_____

_____

_____

_____

_____

_____

_____

_____

_____

_____

_____

_____

_____

_____

_____

*A simple pleasure like a good book gives our imagination
freedom to roam. . .then wander back home.*

Date and Time:

Place:

Today, I found simple inspiration in:

Other inspiring thoughts: _____

_____

_____

_____

_____

_____

_____

_____

_____

_____

_____

_____

_____

_____

_____

_____

_____

_____

_____

_____

_____

_____

How calmly we commit ourselves to the hands
of Him who bears up the world.
JEAN PAUL RICHTER

> *"I am with you and will watch over you wherever you go. . . .*
> *I will not leave you until I have done what I have promised you."*
>
> GENESIS 28:15 NIV

Date and Time:

Place:

Today, I found simple inspiration in:

Other inspiring thoughts: _____

_____

_____

_____

_____

_____

_____

_____

_____

_____

_____

_____

_____

_____

_____

_____

_____

_____

_____

_____

_____

_____

Gratitude is the heart's memory.

FRENCH PROVERB

Trust that any unclear moments will bring you to that moment of clarity and action when you are known by God and know Him. These are the better and brighter moments of His blessing.

UNKNOWN

Date and Time:

Place:

Today, I found simple inspiration in:

Other inspiring thoughts: _____

_____

_____

_____

_____

_____

_____

_____

_____

_____

_____

_____

_____

_____

_____

_____

_____

_____

_____

*A simple pleasure like holding hands conveys to friends
and loved ones that they are God's very best gifts.*

Yet I am always with you; you hold me by my right hand.

PSALM 73:23 NIV

Date and Time:

Place:

Today, I found simple inspiration in:

Other inspiring thoughts: _____

_____

_____

_____

_____

_____

_____

_____

_____

_____

_____

_____

_____

_____

_____

_____

_____

_____

_____

_____

Our greatest experiences are our quietest moments.
FRIEDRICH NIETZSCHE

Earth with her thousand voices, praises God.

SAMUEL TAYLOR COLERIDGE

Date and Time:

Place:

Today, I found simple inspiration in:

Other inspiring thoughts: _____

_____

_____

_____

_____

_____

_____

_____

_____

_____

_____

_____

_____

_____

_____

_____

_____

_____

_____

God hides some ideal in every human soul.
At some time in our life we feel a trembling, fearful longing
to do some good thing. Life finds its noblest spring
of excellence in this hidden impulse to do our best.
ROBERT COLLYER

Finally. . .whatever is true, whatever is noble,
whatever is right, whatever is pure, whatever is lovely,
whatever is admirable—if anything is excellent
or praiseworthy—think about such things.

PHILIPPIANS 4:8 NIV

Date and Time:

Place:

Today, I found simple inspiration in:

Other inspiring thoughts: _____

_Love. . .it begins with a moment that grows richer
and brighter. . .and becomes a lifetime of joy._
UNKNOWN

A simple pleasure like fresh-brewed coffee awakens our minds and thaws our hearts on chilly mornings.

Date and Time:

Place:

Today, I found simple inspiration in:

Other inspiring thoughts: _____

_____

_____

_____

_____

_____

_____

_____

_____

_____

_____

_____

_____

_____

_____

_____

_____

_____

_____

_____

_____

When morning gilds the skies, my heart awakening cries:
May Jesus Christ be praised!
JOSEPH BARNBY

Trust steadily in God, hope unswervingly, love extravagantly.
And the best of the three is love.
1 CORINTHIANS 13:13 MSG

Date and Time:

Place:

Today, I found simple inspiration in:

Other inspiring thoughts: _____

_____

_____

_____

_____

_____

_____

_____

_____

_____

_____

_____

_____

_____

_____

_____

_____

_____

_____

May there always be work for your hands to do.
May your purse always hold a coin or two.
May the sun always shine on your windowpane.
May a rainbow be certain to follow each rain.
May the hand of a friend always be near you, and
May God fill your heart with gladness to cheer you.

IRISH BLESSING

Let my soul take refuge. . .beneath the shadow of Your wings:
let my heart, this sea of restless waves,
find peace in You, O God.
AUGUSTINE

Date and Time:

Place:

Today, I found simple inspiration in:

Other inspiring thoughts: _____

_____

_____

_____

_____

_____

_____

_____

_____

_____

_____

_____

_____

_____

_____

_____

_____

_____

_____

*A simple pleasure like fresh-cut flowers brings
God's exquisite beauty into our lives in any season.*

Date and Time:

Place:

Today, I found simple inspiration in:

Other inspiring thoughts:

_Faith never knows where it is being led,
but it loves and knows the One who is leading._

OSWALD CHAMBERS

To appreciate beauty; to find the best in others; to give one's self; to leave the world a little better, whether by a healthy child, a garden patch, or a redeemed social condition; to have played and laughed with enthusiasm, and sung with exultation; to know even one life has breathed easier because you have lived. . . . This is to have succeeded.

RALPH WALDO EMERSON

Date and Time:

Place:

Today, I found simple inspiration in:

Other inspiring thoughts: _____

_____

_____

_____

_____

_____

_____

_____

_____

_____

_____

_____

_____

_____

_____

_____

_____

_____

_____

_____

_____

_____

The mere sense of living is joy enough.
EMILY DICKINSON

"Only in returning to me and resting in me will you be saved.
In quietness and confidence is your strength."

ISAIAH 30:15 NLT

Date and Time:

Place:

Today, I found simple inspiration in:

Other inspiring thoughts: _____

_____

_____

_____

_____

_____

_____

_____

_____

_____

_____

_____

_____

_____

_____

_____

_____

_____

_____

*A simple pleasure like candlelight makes everything
in its glow radiate love and loveliness.*

God is as great in minuteness as He is in magnitude.

UNKNOWN

Date and Time:

Place:

Today, I found simple inspiration in:

Other inspiring thoughts: _____

_____

_____

_____

_____

_____

_____

_____

_____

_____

_____

_____

_____

_____

_____

_____

_____

_____

_____

_____

_____

_____

All things bright and beautiful, all creatures great and small,
All things wise and wonderful, the Lord God made them all.
CECIL FRANCES ALEXANDER

*Surprise us with love at daybreak; then we'll skip and dance
all the day long. . . . And let the loveliness of our Lord,
our God, rest on us, confirming the work that we do.*

PSALM 90:14, 17 MSG

Date and Time:

Place:

Today, I found simple inspiration in:

Other inspiring thoughts: _____

_____

_____

_____

_____

_____

_____

_____

_____

_____

_____

_____

_____

_____

_____

_____

_____

_____

_____

_____

Always be in a state of expectancy,
and see that you leave room for God to come in as He likes.
OSWALD CHAMBERS

Simple pleasures like early morning solitude renew us
with reverie and plentitude of the soul.

Date and Time:

Place:

Today, I found simple inspiration in:

Other inspiring thoughts: _____

_____

_____

_____

_____

_____

_____

_____

_____

_____

_____

_____

_____

_____

_____

_____

_____

_____

_____

_____

*A simple pleasure like a Sunday afternoon nap
refreshes our bodies and restores our souls.*

For great is your love, higher than the heavens;
your faithfulness reaches to the skies.
Be exalted, O God, above the heavens,
and let your glory be over all the earth.

PSALM 108:4–5 NIV

Date and Time:

Place:

Today, I found simple inspiration in:

Other inspiring thoughts: _____

_A_ simple pleasure like an old favorite song replays
the emotions and memories of sweet days gone by.

Drop Thy still dews of quietness till all our strivings cease;
Take from our souls the strain and stress,
And let our ordered lives confess the beauty of Thy peace.

JOHN GREENLEAF WHITTIER

Date and Time:

Place:

Today, I found simple inspiration in:

Other inspiring thoughts: _____

_____

_____

_____

_____

_____

_____

_____

_____

_____

_____

_____

_____

_____

_____

_____

_____

_____

_____

*We walk without fear, full of hope and courage
and strength to do His will, waiting for the endless good which
He is always giving as fast as He can get us able to take it in.*

GEORGE MACDONALD

Hear my cry, O God; listen to my prayer. From the ends of the earth I call to you, I call as my heart grows faint; lead me to the rock that is higher than I. For you have been my refuge.

PSALM 61:1–3 NIV

Date and Time:

Place:

Today, I found simple inspiration in:

Other inspiring thoughts: _____

_____

_____

_____

_____

_____

_____

_____

_____

_____

_____

_____

_____

_____

_____

_____

_____

_____

Simple pleasures like chocolate chip cookies fresh from the oven are melt-in-your-mouth irresistible!

I like breakfast-time better than any other moment in the day.
No dust has settled on one's mind then,
and it presents a clear mirror to the rays of things.
GEORGE ELIOT

Date and Time:

Place:

Today, I found simple inspiration in:

Other inspiring thoughts: _____

_____

_____

_____

_____

_____

_____

_____

_____

_____

_____

_____

_____

_____

_____

_____

_____

_____

_____

_____

_____

The sun. . .in its full glory, either at rising or setting—
this and many other like blessings we enjoy daily;
and for the most of them, because they are so common,
most men forget to pay their praises. But let us not.
IZAAK WALTON

I know what I'm doing. I have it all planned out—
plans to take care of you, not abandon you,
plans to give you the future you hope for.

JEREMIAH 29:11 MSG

Date and Time:

Place:

Today, I found simple inspiration in:

Other inspiring thoughts: _____

_____
_____
_____
_____
_____
_____
_____
_____
_____
_____
_____
_____
_____
_____
_____
_____
_____
_____
_____
_____

From the simple seeds of childlike faith, we reap the lovely harvest of God's reassuring presence in our lives.

UNKNOWN

Thank you, God for little things that often come our way,
The things we take for granted but don't mention when we pray.
The unexpected courtesy, the thoughtful kindly deed,
A hand reached out to help us in the time of sudden need.

HELEN STEINER RICE

Date and Time:

Place:

Today, I found simple inspiration in:

Other inspiring thoughts: _____

_____

_____

_____

_____

_____

_____

_____

_____

_____

_____

_____

_____

_____

_____

_____

_____

_____

_____

_____

*A simple pleasure like lavender-scented linens
calms our senses as we inhale the savory, clean fragrance.*

That you may know the hope to which he has called you,
the riches of his glorious inheritance in the saints,
and his incomparably great power for us who believe.
That power is like the working of his mighty strength,
which he exerted in Christ when he raised him from the dead.

EPHESIANS 1:18–20 NIV

Date and Time:

Place:

Today, I found simple inspiration in:

Other inspiring thoughts: _____

_____

_____

_____

_____

_____

_____

_____

_____

_____

_____

_____

_____

_____

_____

_____

_____

_____

_____

_____

You have set Your glory above the heavens.
Thy glory flames from sun and star:
Center and soul of every sphere,
Yet to each loving heart how near.
OLIVER WENDELL HOLMES

The God who holds the whole world in His hands wraps Himself in the splendor of the sun's light and walks among the clouds.

UNKNOWN

Date and Time:

Place:

Today, I found simple inspiration in:

Other inspiring thoughts: _____

_____

_____

_____

_____

_____

_____

_____

_____

_____

_____

_____

_____

_____

_____

_____

_____

_____

_____

_____

Contentment is not the fulfillment of what you want,
but the realization of how much you already have.
UNKNOWN

But you, O Lord, are a shield around me. . . .
I lay down and slept, yet I woke up in safety,
for the Lord was watching over me.
PSALM 3:3, 5 NLT

Date and Time:

Place:

Today, I found simple inspiration in:

Other inspiring thoughts: _____

_____

_____

_____

_____

_____

_____

_____

_____

_____

_____

_____

_____

_____

_____

_____

_____

_____

_____

_____

_____

Simple pleasures like Grandfather's stories
undergird us with a shared legacy of love.

*Half the joy of life is in the little things taken on the run.
Let us run if we must. . .but let us keep our hearts young and
our eyes open that nothing worth our while shall escape us. And
everything is worth its while if we only grasp it and its significance.*
CHARLES VICTOR CERBULIEZ

Date and Time:

Place:

Today, I found simple inspiration in:

Other inspiring thoughts:

What we need is not new light, but new sight; not new paths,
but new strength to walk in the old ones; not new duties but new wisdom
from on High to fulfill those that are plain before us.

UNKNOWN

"The LORD your God is with you, he is mighty to save.
He will take great delight in you, he will quiet you with his love,
he will rejoice over you with singing."
ZEPHANIAH 3:17 NIV

Date and Time:

Place:

Today, I found simple inspiration in:

Other inspiring thoughts: _____

_____

_____

_____

_____

_____

_____

_____

_____

_____

_____

_____

_____

_____

_____

_____

_____

*Don't let yourself get so busy that you miss those little
but important extras in life—the beauty of a day. . .the smile
of a friend. . .the serenity of a quiet moment alone.
For it is often life's smallest pleasures and gentlest joys
that make the biggest and most lasting difference.*

UNKNOWN

God's promises are not intended to supersede,
but to excite and encourage our prayers.

MATTHEW HENRY

Date and Time:

Place:

Today, I found simple inspiration in:

Other inspiring thoughts: _____

_A_ simple pleasure like laughter with friends creates
a contagious bond of affection and companionship.

In everything. . .present your requests to God.
And the peace of God, which transcends all understanding,
will guard your hearts and your minds in Christ Jesus.

PHILIPPIANS 4:6–7 NIV

Date and Time:

Place:

Today, I found simple inspiration in:

Other inspiring thoughts: _____

All the world is an utterance of the Almighty.
Its countless beauties, its exquisite adaptations,
all speak to you of Him.

PHILLIPS BROOKS

Love makes burdens lighter, because you divide them.
It makes joys more intense, because you share them.
It makes you stronger, so that you can reach out and
become involved with life in ways you dared not risk alone.

UNKNOWN

Date and Time:

Place:

Today, I found simple inspiration in:

Other inspiring thoughts: _____

_____

_____

_____

_____

_____

_____

_____

_____

_____

_____

_____

_____

_____

_____

_____

_____

_____

_____

_____

_____

I love tranquil solitude
And such society
As is quiet, wise and good.
PERCY BYSSHE SHELLEY

What matters is not your outer appearance. . .
but your inner disposition. Cultivate inner beauty,
the gentle, gracious kind that God delights in.
1 PETER 3:3–4 MSG

Date and Time:

Place:

Today, I found simple inspiration in:

Other inspiring thoughts: _____

_____

_____

_____

_____

_____

_____

_____

_____

_____

_____

_____

_____

_____

_____

_____

_____

_____

_____

_____

_____

This is my Father's world:
I rest me in the thought
Of rocks and trees, of skies and seas;
His hand the wonders wrought.
MALTBIE D. BABCOCK

A simple pleasure like sunshine after a storm illuminates the image of clouds in our lives giving way to clear, open skies.

Date and Time:

Place:

Today, I found simple inspiration in:

Other inspiring thoughts: _____

_____

_____

_____

_____

_____

_____

_____

_____

_____

_____

_____

_____

_____

_____

_____

_____

_____

_____

_____

_____

There are no little things.
Little things, so called, are the hinges of the universe.
FANNY FERN

Date and Time:

Place:

Today, I found simple inspiration in:

Other inspiring thoughts: _____

_____

_____

_____

_____

_____

_____

_____

_____

_____

_____

_____

_____

_____

_____

_____

_____

_____

_____

_____

_____

_____

May your life become one of glad and unending praise
to the Lord as you journey through this world,
and in the world that is to come!
TERESA OF AVILA

Although it is good to think upon the kindness of God
and to love Him and worship Him for it,
yet it is far better to gaze upon the pure essence of Him
and to love Him and worship Him for himself.

UNKNOWN

Date and Time:

Place:

Today, I found simple inspiration in:

Other inspiring thoughts: _____

_____

_____

_____

_____

_____

_____

_____

_____

_____

_____

_____

_____

_____

_____

_____

_____

_____

_____

_____

*May God send His love like sunshine in His warm
and gentle way, to fill each corner
of your heart each moment of today.*

UNKNOWN

Trust in the LORD with all your heart;
do not depend on your own understanding.
Seek his will in all you do, and he will show you which path to take.

PROVERBS 3:5–6 NLT

Date and Time:

Place:

Today, I found simple inspiration in:

Other inspiring thoughts:

*A simple pleasure like a conversation with a good friend
is far more significant than its simplicity might suggest.*

And if tonight my soul may find her peace in sleep,
and sink in good oblivion, and in the morning wake
like a new-opened flower, then I have been
dipped again in God, and new created.

D. H. LAWRENCE

Date and Time:

Place:

Today, I found simple inspiration in:

Other inspiring thoughts: _____

_____

_____

_____

_____

_____

_____

_____

_____

_____

_____

_____

_____

_____

_____

_____

_____

_____

_____

_____

_____

_____

Only God gives true peace—a quiet gift He sets within us
just when we think we've exhausted our search for it.
UNKNOWN

*"Though the mountains be shaken and the hills be removed,
yet my unfailing love for you will not be shaken nor my covenant
of peace be removed," says the LORD, who has compassion on you.*

ISAIAH 54:10 NIV

Date and Time:

Place:

Today, I found simple inspiration in:

Other inspiring thoughts: _____

We are born to have connection with God.
CLEMENT OF ALEXANDRIA

*The soul should always stand ajar,
ready to welcome the ecstatic experience.*

EMILY DICKINSON

Date and Time:

Place:

Today, I found simple inspiration in:

Other inspiring thoughts: _____

_____
_____
_____
_____
_____
_____
_____
_____
_____
_____
_____
_____
_____
_____
_____
_____
_____
_____
_____
_____
_____

A simple pleasure like a star-studded sky reveals God's glory with awesome clarity and humbling majesty.

*God is our refuge and strength, an ever-present help in trouble.
Therefore we will not fear, though the earth give way
and the mountains fall into the heart of the sea. . . .
The Lord Almighty is with us.*

PSALM 46:1–2, 7 NIV

Date and Time:

Place:

Today, I found simple inspiration in:

Other inspiring thoughts: _____

_____

_____

_____

_____

_____

_____

_____

_____

_____

_____

_____

_____

_____

_____

_____

_____

_____

_____

_____

The year's at the spring
And day's at the morn. . . .
God's in His heaven—
All's right with the world!
ROBERT BROWNING

The greatest honor we can give God is to live gladly because of the knowledge of His love.

JULIAN OF NORWICH

Date and Time:

Place:

Today, I found simple inspiration in:

Other inspiring thoughts: _____

_____

_____

_____

_____

_____

_____

_____

_____

_____

_____

_____

_____

_____

_____

_____

_____

_____

_____

_____

What is a home? A roof to keep out the rain?
Four walls to keep out the wind? Floors to keep out the cold?
Yes, but home is more than that. It is the laugh of a baby,
the warmth of loving hearts, lights from happy eyes, kindness,
loyalty, comradeship. . . . That is home. God bless it.

UNKNOWN

The LORD longs to be gracious to you; he rises to show you compassion.
For the LORD is a God of justice.
Blessed are all who wait for him!
ISAIAH 30:18 NIV

Date and Time:

Place:

Today, I found simple inspiration in:

Other inspiring thoughts: _____

_____

_____

_____

_____

_____

_____

_____

_____

_____

_____

_____

_____

_____

_____

_____

_____

_____

_____

_____

_____

_____

How beautiful it is to be alive! To wake each morn as if the Maker's grace did us afresh from nothingness derive, that we might sing "How happy is our case! How beautiful it is to be alive!"
HENRY SEPTIMUS SUTTON

*A simple pleasure like a fiery sunset is
God's spectacular signature on the horizon.*

Date and Time:

Place:

Today, I found simple inspiration in:

Other inspiring thoughts: _____

_____

_____

_____

_____

_____

_____

_____

_____

_____

_____

_____

_____

_____

_____

_____

_____

_____

_____

_____

_____

The seed of joy grows best in a field of peace.
ROBERT J. WICKS

Submit yourselves, then, to God. . . .
Come near to God and he will come near to you.
JAMES 4:7–8 NIV

Date and Time:

Place:

Today, I found simple inspiration in:

Other inspiring thoughts: _____

_____
_____
_____
_____
_____
_____
_____
_____
_____
_____
_____
_____
_____
_____
_____
_____
_____
_____
_____
_____
_____

The gift of life unwraps itself through time;
all we need to do is sit back and enjoy its contents.
UNKNOWN

Simple pleasures like muted night sounds whisper to our souls, "Peace. Be still."

Date and Time:

Place:

Today, I found simple inspiration in:

Other inspiring thoughts: _____

_The fruit of our placing all things in His hands is
the presence of His abiding peace in our hearts._

HANNAH WHITALL SMITH

For God, who said, "Let light shine out of darkness,"
made his light shine in our hearts to give us the light of
the knowledge of the glory of God in the face of Christ.
2 CORINTHIANS 4:6 NIV

Date and Time:

Place:

Today, I found simple inspiration in:

Other inspiring thoughts: _____

_____

_____

_____

_____

_____

_____

_____

_____

_____

_____

_____

_____

_____

_____

_____

_____

_____

_____

_____

_____

*A rainbow stretches from one end of the sky to the other.
Each shade of color, each facet of light, displays the radiant
spectrum of God's love—a promise that He will always
love each one of us at our worst and at our best.*

UNKNOWN

A simple pleasure like moonlight reflects God's bright glory across the backdrop of the heavens.

Date and Time:

Place:

Today, I found simple inspiration in:

Other inspiring thoughts: _____

_____

_____

_____

_____

_____

_____

_____

_____

_____

_____

_____

_____

_____

_____

_____

_____

_____

_____

_____

_____

*How can you expect God to speak in that gentle and inward
voice which melts the soul, when you are making so much noise. . . ?
Be silent and God will speak again.*

FRANÇOIS FÉNELON

The LORD pours down his blessings.
Our land will yield its bountiful harvest.
PSALM 85:12 NLT

Date and Time:

Place:

Today, I found simple inspiration in:

Other inspiring thoughts: _____

_A simple pleasure like a porch swing lulls our spirits
with the restful rhythms of God's grace._

Into all our lives, in many simple, familiar, homely ways,
God infuses this element of joy from the surprises of life,
which unexpectedly brighten our days and fill our eyes with light.
HENRY WADSWORTH LONGFELLOW

Date and Time:

Place:

Today, I found simple inspiration in:

Other inspiring thoughts: _____

_____

_____

_____

_____

_____

_____

_____

_____

_____

_____

_____

_____

_____

_____

_____

_____

_____

_____

_____

We may. . .depend upon God's promises, for. . .
He will be as good as His word. He is so kind that He cannot
deceive us, so true that He cannot break His promise.

MATTHEW HENRY

Date and Time:

Place:

Today, I found simple inspiration in:

Other inspiring thoughts: _____

_____

_____

_____

_____

_____

_____

_____

_____

_____

_____

_____

_____

_____

_____

_____

_____

_____

_____

_____

Not knowing when the dawn will come,
I open every door.
EMILY DICKINSON

A simple pleasure like a dew-kissed morning offers this fresh day, this new chance of life, as a gift from God.

Date and Time:

Place:

Today, I found simple inspiration in:

Other inspiring thoughts: _____

_____

_____

_____

_____

_____

_____

_____

_____

_____

_____

_____

_____

_____

_____

_____

_____

_____

_____

_____

*A simple pleasure like a rainbow illustrates God's
everlasting faithfulness encircling all the earth.*

The LORD is my shepherd; I shall not want.
He maketh me to lie down in green pastures:
he leadeth me beside the still waters. He restoreth my soul.

PSALM 23:1–3 KJV

Date and Time:

Place:

Today, I found simple inspiration in:

Other inspiring thoughts:

*Let your life be distinguished by conscientious work,
by graciousness, by simple kindness, and above all,
by a readiness to serve.*

UNKNOWN

A simple pleasure like wildflowers scatters untamed beauty across the landscape of our hearts.

Date and Time:

Place:

Today, I found simple inspiration in:

Other inspiring thoughts:

*A simple pleasure like the unconditional love of a dog
reminds us that though we may stray,
God always calls us back to the home of His heart.*

*The eternal God is your refuge,
and underneath are the everlasting arms.*
DEUTERONOMY 33:27 NIV

Date and Time:

Place:

Today, I found simple inspiration in: